FLY GIRLS: Three Biographies of Female
Aviation Pioneers

Stories of Bessie Coleman, Dr Ola Brown
(née Orekunrin) and Kimberly Anyadike

Amanda Epe

FLY GIRLS: Three Biographies of Female Aviation Pioneers

Stories of Bessie Coleman, Dr Ola Brown (née Orekunrin) and Kimberly Anyadike

by

Amanda Epe

Blossom Books

LONDON

BLOSSOM BOOKS

First published in Great Britain
by Blossom Books.

Copyright © Amanda Epe 2021
Amanda Epe asserts the moral right to be
identified as the author of this work.
A catalogue record of this book is available
from the British Library.

ISBN 9781838302511

This work is a work of fiction with a small number of character names changed or created based on the true stories and lives of Bessie Coleman, Dr Ola Brown and Kimberly Anyadike.

Two stories are written in American English and one in British English.

All rights reserved. No part of this publication may be reproduced, stored in a retrieval system, or transmitted, in any form or by any means, electronic, mechanical, photocopying, recording or otherwise, without the prior permission of the publishers.

'Dream, fly, let your imagination take you high.'

~ Amanda Epe

This book is for sisters and those who know the power of sisterhood. These stories show the love of sister bonding.

Acknowledgements

To all the readers of my debut book *A Fly Girl* who have requested to read more of my writing and my writing buddies, I acknowledge you. To all the children and young people I've met in schools – you inspire me to write for children. As always, I give a massive thanks to my family for their continuous encouragement. Thanks to the TLC Agency for professional support, reader Antonia Prescott for her golden guidance and to all the editors. Thanks to Sam Wall, who has got me covered, designing epic covers and illustrations.

Table of Contents

Acknowledgements............................7

She Dreamed, Dared and Did............11
    Chapter 1.......................................12
    Chapter 2.......................................34
    Chapter 3.......................................41

Rescue in the Skies 51
    Chapter 1.......................................52
    Chapter 2.......................................62
    Chapter 3.......................................70

Around the States in 13 Days............79
    Diary 1..80
    Diary 2..87
    Dairy 3..96
    Note...101

Five Facts...102
Quick Quiz...108

She Dreamed, Dared and Did: Bessie Coleman

Chapter One

Mama Coleman soothed Bessie's sore feet, massaging them from the four-mile daily walk to school and back. It was a Friday evening and the miles had accumulated. The relaxing massage allowed her mind to wander. She loved to dream. *If only I could fly*

and give my poor feet a break. They need a rest from the walking, she had thought. Most children would have missed a day or two but not Bessie Coleman. Bessie loved learning and she excelled in everything she was taught. She mastered all her subjects and was ahead in her mathematics lessons.

"This is a compass. Look, I've written it down. Say C-c-c-om..." Bessie was showing her young sisters her mathematics set.

Susan Coleman's eyebrows rose as she looked at the school letter. She scratched her scalp between the neatly placed black cornrowed hairstyle, before continuing to massage her daughter's feet.

"I need to buy a math set. The letter says that the school can lend me this one for a week, but I need to buy my own."

"Yes, Bess my darling. God will provide us money for you to have your very own," her mother said.

Bessie would regularly help her parents read after school. They were unable to read because they had not been allowed to attend school. Although her parents had been born free to slaved parents, the laws did not allow enslaved people to read and write. Bessie was the first of her family to become literate, and she helped others in her family understand the meanings of words.

"Bessie, it's my turn! That was my jam," Georgia yelled, as they scooped turn by turn the cornmeal porridge

Mama had made for them. "Mama, when can I have my own bowl? Bessie ate all my jam!"

Bessie slowed down. She knew she had gobbled up their favourite snack desperately. The trudge home from the one-room schoolhouse had weakened Bessie, draining her energy and toughening her toes as she trekked. But she still had a soft spot for her little sister. "You can finish the rest of the porridge, and I've left you the big blob of jam." Bessie felt a twinge in her stomach and heard it groan for three minutes. The massage Mama had given her had kissed the surface of the pain in her feet, and the food had filled a tiny space in her stomach. She needed to lie down. "Thank you, Mama. My feet feel better, and the porridge was tasty." She excused herself from the table to the far corner of the room.

Elois and Nilus had eaten before Bessie. Her brothers John, Isaiah and Walter were next to share the bowl and sit around the tiny table. The eldest, Lilah and Alberta, always waited patiently for the last of the siblings to eat. They helped their mother churn the cornmeal and wash the plates after each group had finished. The thirteen children huddled together to eat, live, laugh, learn and sleep. Their echoes expanded and enlivened the tiny living room.

It was a frosty night. The Coleman children draped themselves in blankets, told stories and played. The aroma of sweet cinnamon in the porridge and the steam from the stew

Mama was cooking brought warmth to their shelter.

"Catch the bean bag, Bessie!" John chucked it over to Isaiah, and they threw it back and forth.

"*You gonna* be piggy in the middle forever, Bess," Isaiah teased. Bessie's face twisted up. She didn't want to catch the bean bag or play any of their games, but her brothers didn't get it. They were happy to play.

"Wait Bess, let's play one more game before you go to your room," John pleaded.

John was really happy that Dad had moved them to Waxahachie, Texas and built a house with three rooms because he remembered how they had used to live.

"Put the ball down NOW, John! Everyone needs to sleep." Papa Coleman would raise his voice, as John made a racket in the dirt-floored one-room cabin they had previously lived in. John would bounce his ball as it pounded harshly onto the bare floorboards.

On this particular night, when Bessie was beaten down and famished, the last thing she wanted to do was play. As darkness set in, and the distant street lamp flickered on and off, Bessie knew she wouldn't be able to read over her schoolbooks until the light of day on Saturday morning.

"Good night Lilah, Alberta, Bess, Georgia and Elois, and remember to say your own prayers." Mama had said the Lord's Prayer with them and individually kissed them goodnight, blowing the lamp out before she left their room.

*****

The family was very close to each other, supporting each other through tough times. The Coleman children had lost one of their siblings. The death of the small child had hit the family hard, and they were deeply saddened. George Coleman, their father, was disturbed about the racial discrimination. He and his wife could not get jobs, and it pained him to watch his children work picking crops in the fields. He felt it was better to move away from Texas to Indian land.

"I counted that I picked about a thousand crops this morning," Bessie had once said to her dad before settling down to do her homework. Papa Coleman ran his hands through his long, jet-black hair dangling over his face and scowled. George's head hung downwards often, and he had become more reserved as he watched his children work hard in the fields.

Then, suddenly, he abandoned the home when Bessie was nine years old.

*****

"Mama is always crying," Georgia said to Bessie one day as soon as her big sister returned from school. The family had suffered too much sadness. So, Bessie made her mind up to make it her duty to support her mother and care for her younger sisters, who looked up to her.

At home, Bessie felt unmotivated. She missed her dad and wished she could see him again. He had not been back since he had left home and returned to his mother's native land in Oklahoma.

One night, Bessie went to bed. She curled up and faced away from Georgia, as tiny teardrops rolled down her cheeks and soaked into the blanket. Bessie wiped her eyes and fell into a deep slumber immediately. It had been an exhausting week. She realized her dad was not coming back and feared she would not see him again.

"I've heard you, little Beth, today, yesterday and for some time now in your dreams," said Grandma T. Bessie's mother's mother used to call her the shortened version of her full name, Elizabeth. Her grandmother spoke to Bessie in her dreams about watching over her from her place away from this earth and assured her that better days were to come.

"You will fly my dear. Yes, you will be the first official flyer. I had a dream when I was a slave child that my children's children will be free. Free to fly!"

"Nana, how will I fly?" Bessie asked. But before long, Grandma T disappeared, and Bessie's mind wandered into another dream.

"Bessie, you will be the first Cherokee woman to fly an aircraft, and you will make us proud," Grandma Coleman smiled at her. Bessie saw a photo of her grandma sitting next to her son George. Bessie was too excited in her dream. She saw her dad again, even though it was just a picture.

Her maternal grandma talked about flying, flying to be free from the chains of slavery. Her paternal grandmother told her that she would make her native American family proud of standing up for her rights as an indigenous American woman and fulfilling her dreams.

"An airplane! But Grandma, how will I do this?" Bessie exclaimed.

Bessie continued to dream. Sometimes her grandmothers talked to her, and other times, it was ancestors she had never met introducing themselves to her. They told her that she had been sent to bring justice to their people. They had suffered during their time on earth, and she was the progeny to bring hope to women and Black people in America.

*****

"Yes, Bessie, tell us the answer," her teacher asked her again, as she put her hand up to all the math questions asked. After school, Bessie walked home and told her friends that she loved her lessons and maybe she'll become a pilot one day. The girls giggled. Never had they seen either a woman or a Black person fly a plane.

"I'm not imagining this. Both of my grandmothers have told me the same story," Bessie tried to explain.

Bessie could not understand her dreams, and the more she tried to ignore them, the more dreams she had. She once dreamed that she was flying an aircraft in a land far away. Mama, unlike her friends, believed that the ancestors were speaking to Bessie, reminding her that African people believed in listening to ancestral voices. She woke up one morning remembering speaking words in another language, though she hadn't been taught another language in school. Bessie would be whisked away on a rollercoaster ride on some nights. Other nights she felt the thrills of the circus, but she was way above ground level. In most of her dreams, she hovered around in the blue sky, floating and feeling light. Many nights the frequent reoccurring dreams of flying an aircraft returned. She thought this must be because her grandmothers had put the idea in her head. But she also was fascinated every time she saw an aircraft soar above her head when walking to school and remembered that her mother said that our ancestors do speak to us.

Chapter Two

Bessie embraced Georgia. They hugged each other for a good while. Like magnets, they remained bonded, keeping everyone waiting when other family members came to say bye and hug Bessie.

"*I'm gonna miss y'all,*" Bessie said emotionally, but the dancing made her look happy. She hosted her eighteen birthday and farewell party. It was time to leave Texas and her beloved family. She had done the family proud by gaining a scholarship to university to study math in Oklahoma where her father came from. She had exceeded in her studies in elementary and high school, and her dreams were starting to look real.

*****

Life was great, and Bessie passed her first year of university with flying colours. One day, Bessie was pacing up and down, tearing her hair out while reading a letter.

I gotta be crazy, believing in hearing my grandmas' voices and dreaming of flying. Bessie started to doubt her vision when the news came to inform her that she couldn't go on to the second year of university because she couldn't afford the tuition fees. Bessie was saddened. Her dream to complete a university education was shattered. She had asked for support from people in the community and from charities, but nothing was available.

"You'll find a good job, Bessie. You went to university so a lot of companies will accept you," Georgia comforted her. Bessie wanted to help her younger sisters to study, but the news set back her plans to support her family. She came to realize that she had no choice but to start looking for any opportunity to work and decided to move in with her brothers.

*****

"You can start tomorrow," the manager of the salon said. The city of Chicago was dazzling, a tremendous shift from the simple southern life Bessie had grown up in. She worked as a manicurist and enjoyed the artistic way she designed the nails and pampered the women. She was happy earning some money, helping her family and having fun living with her brothers who had returned from the First World War. But she secretly had a dream that was unfulfilled. Her brothers knew what Bessie had always dreamed of doing and told her that in France women were flying aircraft, and colour was not a barrier.

Chapter Three

Chapter Three

Busy Bessie had left her brothers and was seeking a purpose in life. Life in Chicago was exciting: she had connected with African American leaders and made valuable networks.

"You are a determined young woman, Bessie. Have you ever thought about flying? You seem so brave," Robert Abbott asked. Before Bessie could question any further, Robert shared his visions. "Go to France and learn to be a pilot, and when you return, I'll publish you on the front cover of my paper."

Bessie trusted that Robert would sponsor her, but she still worked privately, gaining her own clients as a manicurist.

"Of course, Bessie, in my country women are allowed to fly, and we have several Black pilots training," said Antonia, a fashionable French middle-aged lady, filling Bessie's head with the best news.

"This is incredible! What do I have to do? I really can't believe it. What is the entry age?" Bessie had numerous questions.

Antonia blew her nails dry and smiled at Bessie's artwork. "Well, at first we better get you to speak French, *tu comprends?*"

Bessie knew this coincidence was the key to her destiny. Shortly after

Robert offered to sponsor her, she met a French client. Antonia. She knew she was on the right pathway. Her childhood dreams hadn't been in vain. Her mission was clear. She started to learn French in the evenings after work, and in no time, she was a fluent speaker. She then began taking examinations to apply for the piloting program in France. She was selected and went to live and train to be a pilot in France.

*****

Bessie obtained her pilot's license on June 15, 1921 and returned to

America to be the first Black American and Cherokee woman with an international license. She became a star and was asked to perform her flying skills in exhibitions.

"Hey, I've done it again!" Bessie frequently appeared in newspaper headlines. "I want to help other women to fly, Georgia. There's so much freedom in the air, you know".

"But we still don't feel free here in America. We aren't allowed in certain venues, and we are living in racial segregation. The fight for equality is the most important thing for us right now," Georgia said.

Georgia had touched Bessie, and Bessie knew she had to help her people. The lives of Black people mattered to her deeply. This disturbed her, and she refused to perform her aviation tricks unless Black people were allowed to be spectators also and use the same gate as the white people. Her stunts were incredible, and she earned a lot of income from her air shows.

"I think it's time to open an air school for Black people to be able to fly," Bessie told her flight mechanic William Wills. She had achieved her success after many failures and wanted to share her skills with other women. She taught several women in private lessons, and her next goal was to embark on her major dream of a flight school. "I see it based in Atlanta, Texas. Wouldn't it be nice to be in my birthplace, or how about in Chicago, Will?"

"This is the best idea ever, Bessie. After our practice this evening, let's make an official plan of action," Will replied, as they conversed about the flying school. They spent the morning writing notes on where the school would be located, the cost of running it and when it would open.

"Let's go and fly now," Bessie said. After a long afternoon of brainstorming and writing goals, they were feeling on top of the world. They were so delighted and in the highest of spirits. Still laughing together, they walked down to the aerodrome. Will and Bessie climbed into the aircraft and disappeared over the horizon into the setting sun.

*****

That day in 1926 was the last time anyone saw Bessie, aged 34. Although her dream of opening up a flying school was never realized, her memory lives on: she was the catalyst and inspiration for African American aviators.

Rescue In The Skies: Dr Ola Brown
(née Orekunrin)

Chapter One

One sunny day, two sisters were playing at the beach, dipping their sandy brown toes in the aqua waters. The girls loved the trek from their fishing town to the coast of Lowestoft. It was a beautiful beach resort of wide sandy shores.

They splashed about in the waves after building mini sandcastles. Ola saw how her younger sister's eyes illuminated like stars when they played together. So, she nicknamed her Twinkle.

"Catch me if you can, Twinkle," Ola called to her younger sister, as she ran to edge of the low current to cool off.

They had played at length that day and enjoyed their playtime, as normally they worked extra hard at school. The thick sand pasted along their calves made their legs heavy and weary. They were desperate to get back home and were glad their foster dad picked them up. The sandy sludge and speckles on their thighs made the car seats murky. But they were too adventurous to notice and were engrossed in quizzes on the ride home.

They loved going to the seaside and went often as it was very local to them, and there wasn't much else to do in town. Sometimes, all the three biological sisters went together to enjoy the beach glaring into the clear blue skies. Their foster mother added local trips to their schedule to help them, and all the other children in the foster home, explore nature and enjoy the free things in life in their rural town.

"Twinkle, are you feeling okay?" Ola rubbed her sister's back as Twinkle yawned over and over again. Twinkle's smooth brown skin looked an unusual matt tone, and the sparkle in her eyes gradually faded on the journey home. At the beach, she had raced with Wendy, their foster sister, who was sitting in the front of the car with their dad as they drove home.

"I bet Mr Mingle is still working, marking our books," Wendy pointed out as they passed their school that stood silently on the corner like a haunted house. On normal schooldays, Monday to Friday, three forms of pupils crammed into one class. Neither Ola nor Twinkle answered Wendy. Ola was focused on Twinkle's heavy breathing. The girls were so close. Ola always went the extra mile to take care of her sister, who was quite ill with sickle cell anaemia, often feeling tired and weak.

Ola always made her feel like a champion, allowing her to win their races at the beach and family quizzes at home. This particular day, she had won, beating both Ola and the race with Wendy. These moments were treasured, as it wasn't always possible to play together due to Twinkle taking ill and needing rest.

The sisters stood out living in an all-white environment. They were the only Black people in their town and lived with a white foster family. The Orekunrin family originally came from Nigeria, West Africa, and they dreamed of going there one day and meeting all their extended family.

Ronke was delighted to see her sisters return from a fun day at the beach. After family dinner, she helped Twinkle change into her nightclothes and tuck her in. Ola, Twinkle and Ronke stayed up in their room, chatting through to the early hours that night.

"We will eat our most delicious and best food, fried plantain, and bask in the sunshine," Ronke fantasised.

Ola felt excited and remembered stories their biological parents told them when they stayed over with them. "Uncle Tunde will take you on a tour and fly you around from Kano to Lagos to Port Harcourt."

It was astounding to hear of their relatives owning airlines and industries. Where the sisters lived was derelict, with limited opportunities for young people after leaving school. Although it wasn't too exciting in their hometown, the three musketeers made the best of life, and being together made life all the more enjoyable.

Chapter Two

The sisters travelled to Nigeria, and Twinkle became very ill on the trip. She was staying in a remote village far away from any hospital, and therefore, the family couldn't take her to get treatment. She grew weaker. There was no road access, and the only way for Twinkle to receive care was to be transported by an air ambulance, but this country didn't have these facilities or services.

Sadly, Twinkle passed away and left the world, returning home to the skies. Like fragments of broken glass, Ola was shattered. She was deeply distraught that her best friend, her treasured younger sister, was no longer with her. Life had lost its spark without Twinkle. This was the toughest thing Ola had had to experience in her young life. She would look to the skies every night in memory of how the sisters would stay up chatting under the beams of light piercing through their window. Ronke reminisced how the three musketeers would wiggle in the sand on beach trips as the magic wands of sunlight nourished their skin with vitamins. They always looked to the skies and felt nature was a blessing.

"I was about to sleep, but these beautiful stars have given me energy. They've kept me up," Ola said to Ronke as they comforted each other.

"Ola, the energy is in the universe. We've got to listen to what it tells us."

Ola was alert. She was driven. She felt that Twinkle had never really left her, and although it had been the most difficult time for the family, Ola was filled with purpose. *Why weren't there any rescue services in Nigeria to save her sister and others?*

From that night on, Ola rescheduled her time wisely. "Can I borrow more than six books this week?" she would plead with the librarian on each weekend afternoon visit.

"Ah, I see this week you're reading African history," Mr Perkins smiled handing over her books and library card. She read voraciously – aviation books, astronomy, science and business books.

"Ola, we haven't seen you in the evening for ages. Are you hanging out with us on Friday? We're watching a film," their closest foster sister asked as she walked past the living room heading towards her bedroom. Although Ola loved people, time was really valuable, so she selected which social events were the most important to her. It was this mindset and work ethic that had made her studious. Older foster children who had already left the foster home complained about the lack of future prospects when they visited. *But surely life can't be that dismal. My dream is away from here, and Africa is a land of opportunities. I must work hard,* Ola thought.

No one in the area went to university, and it was disheartening to know that education ended at sixteen years old for the young people in her foster home and in the town.

Nature gave and it took away. Ola had learned a lot through her young adolescent life. She knew that if she didn't open her hands, she wouldn't receive what life had to offer her.

Chapter Three

Ola celebrated her fifteenth birthday with the good news that she was going to start university at 15 years old. Her hard work had paid off. She thought differently to the local people and the children in her home that believed there were no prospects. The loss of Twinkle knocked her down, but she had had to pick herself up again, not only to continue life but to help other sick children and people: this was her calling.

"Congratulations! I knew you could do it." Ronke and all the other young people were proud that Ola had achieved her goal. They too were inspired to do something of interest to them. Ola had chosen the right pathway. This pathway would help so many people.

"One day, you'll help so many people, Ola, if you continue your studies in medicine," Ola remembered one of her uncles encouraging her on his visit to England from Nigeria. She thought she'd be working in aviation as she loved planes, but her relatives encouraged her to stick with medicine, and with her sister's passing, she knew what she had to do – work in aviation medicine.

From that night onwards, Ola worked harder and harder and completed her studies way ahead of anyone in the country. She was the youngest medical graduate in England.

But on the night of graduation, as she toasted with her peers, she gazed up and suddenly saw shining skies. She winked at the glimmers above her. From that moment, Ola knew it was time to help. It was time to rescue people by working in the skies.

*****

A few years went by, and Ola moved to Nigeria. It was a tough decision as she had never lived in the country, and she was making progress with the British Medical Association and within a political party. But she had to honour her calling and start her rescue work. It was time to leave her birth nation, England.

Ola was afraid. She had no money to start such a major project, and it was an enormous task that had not been done before. But she believed in starting small and starting from somewhere. Every night, Ola brainstormed and created plans to begin the project. She worked hard getting work experience in medical rescue teams, training in aviation medicine and travelling the world to work in different nations. She was even awarded a scholarship to study in Japan.

Having travelled globally, her fears disappeared about living in Nigeria.

"Tell us about your experience in fundraising, and how do you expect this venture to start?" Mr Suleiman, Director of Finance at Premier Bank in Lagos asked her on her thirtieth investors interview.

"In my undergraduate years, I sold products to help me pay for my university fees, and I succeeded in completing my course. I can afford to hire one aircraft now, and in years to come, the income will grow to buy more." Ola went around Nigeria networking and trying to raise funds to start her business. Ola had become a pilot and, coupled with her medical background, she established the Flying Doctors. Not long after she progressed and bought 20 aircrafts. The helicopter and airplane service has successfully helped and rescued people in Nigeria and all over Africa for over ten years. Ola is now a pioneer in healthcare investment in West Africa. Ola always looks at the skies and is thankful to the many stars guiding her on her journey. She is especially grateful to the team of physicians and her operational staff for being a rescue in the skies.

Around the States in 13 Days: Kimberly Anyadike

Diary One

June 7, 2006

Dear Diary,

I was the happiest girl in the world today, and I can't believe my life, but I was scared. My heart was beating really fast, and my legs were wobbling like Jell-O, but hey, there really wasn't anything to be frightened of. We weren't ~~aloud~~ allowed to fly the planes today. We met our ~~instructures~~ instructors, and they told us the rules. That's so BORING!!! I can't wait to whiz around my school. That's ~~gonna~~ going to be so cool, whizzing over my classroom. I'm glad Mommy came with me today. Maybe next ~~weak~~ week I gets to go by myself. Carly, my new friend who lives not far away from here, sat next to me, and she is also 12, yay! Xoxo

June 14, 2006

Dear Diary,

I've been at flight school one week. They are so strict. They read my writing and say I have too many crossing's out and spelling mistakes, and pilots have to be able to write well. I have to take the rules really seriously or I could lose my place. One of the important rules is to do well at school.

Carly is my new bestie because we have so much in common. She swims, dances and loves many sports too. She lives about one mile away from me in the south of downtown Compton so hopefully I'm going to be learning with her.

August 16, 2006

Dear Diary,

I've been so busy that I've had no time to write about life, but my days at flight school are awesome. I really love it. Mom says I've changed. She says the school has disciplined me. I do my homework straight after school and then learn the aviation topics. I have learned so much since I started. Last week we had a test on everything we had learned in two months, and boy, I was really worried because I don't want to lose my place. I'm glad I passed. Mom would really be upset with me if not.

This fall I'm going to be the best at school. Mom wants me to learn anatomy, and I'm going to do a new timetable for my schoolwork and my aviation lessons. I was so lucky they gave me a job over the summer break. Carly and I splashed each other with the foam when the manager wasn't looking. It was fun cleaning the planes and dusting around the museum. One day soon, we are going to fly those planes, whoopee!

Diary Two

March 13, 2009

Dear Diary,

Today was a success! I got news that my plan to fly around the USA in the summer is going to be permitted. It's almost as if I'm flying solo, but I'm going to be with a safety pilot, Ronnel Norman. I couldn't believe my eyes when I read the letter after school.

Carly came over, and we had a dance-off in my room to celebrate. She's the best hip-hop dancer ever, and she's so fly. I'm so excited and I can't sleep.

March 20, 2009

Dear Diary,

I'm so happy for Kelly today. She is sweet 16, and she is so excited about her letter. She's going to fly four different aircraft in one day. My sister gets to be a pilot before me. Oh well, she's older, but I must do something special too!

June 29, 2009

Dear Diary,

This day truly has been the most incredible day of my life. My dream has come true. I have started my mission to go from one coast and fly across all of the USA. I couldn't believe I was in control when I took off. I wanted to pinch myself meeting Major Levi H. Thornhill. I remembered reading about his service as part of the Tuskegee Airmen. He loves flying even though he's a retired US Airforce pilot. Major Thornhill will be with me throughout the journey. Am I not the luckiest girl in the world?

June 30, 2009

Dear Diary,

I managed to get through another day. I'm more nervous now than excited. We talked about weather conditions. Maybe it's just warnings from the briefing office. I hope my plan can continue.

July 4, 2009

Dear Diary,

This has been the hardest test of time. I'm so tired. It's been five days of flying fun, but I really am exhausted. It's Independence Day, but there's no time for celebration right now.

July 6, 2009

Dear Diary,

I felt like a conqueror today as I manoeuvred through turbulence and kept the plane under control.

July 9, 2009

Dear Diary,

I have flown across beautiful terrains – such epic views of the Arizona desert – and soared across the sea. The best moments are after landing the aircraft, as I'm minutes away from meeting my heroes that I had read about. Major Thornhill has introduced me to the regional chapters of airmen, and my plane has been autographed by about fifty of them already. I'm on cloud nine, having met these African

American pilots who fought in the Second World War. They were true fighters in my eyes, as they fought for our country despite it not accepting African Americans and having systems of racial segregation in place. They fought for their own place and rights in our nation. This was the highlight of my travels. I read about them during Black History Month, and now, I get to meet them. It's because of people like them that I live my piloting dreams.

July 10, 2009

Dear Diary,

My mission is almost over. I'm nearing completion, and I'm lost for words. I finish tomorrow!

Diary Three

September 3, 2009

Dear Diary,

It's a new year at school. Life has been good, so I feel like writing about it especially today as we met Governor Arnold Schwarzenegger, and he awarded Kelly and me at the California State Capitol. Kelly was awarded for being the youngest African American woman piloting four different aircraft in a single day, and I'm the youngest to travel across America in a single-engine Cessna 172. I hope other children will also be driven to say that they can do what the Anyadike sisters have done or follow their own dream. It was worth it that we went to Tomorrow's Aeronautical Museum (TAM). I would never have guessed that when I filled out TAM's application form for disadvantaged kids to fly all those years ago, I would end up here. I was just bored at 12 years old and wanted something to do after school. It changed our lives, and now I believe if I put my mind to something and work hard, anything is possible.

January 1, 2010

Dear Diary,

I didn't write any New Year's resolutions today to share with the family, but we had a lovely dinner at home and a great day. This year I'll be 16. I want to do something different every month. So far, I know I'll be having a big birthday party, even though it's meant to be a surprise.

May 10, 2010

Dear Diary,

Not able to journal as much these days. I'm too busy studying.

*****

Note:

Kimberly graduated from the University of California in 2016, majoring in physiological science and African American studies. She volunteered as a Flying Samaritan to bring medical care to Tijuana in Mexico.

Five Facts About Bessie Coleman

1. Bessie Coleman attended a small, segregated school when she was young.

2. Bessie worked in the cotton fields, as well as going to school.

3. Bessie's school only had one room.

4. Bessie's nicknames were Queen Bess or Brave Bessie.

5. Bessie travelled to the Netherlands and Germany after obtaining her license from France to advance her pilot studies.

Five Facts About Dr Ola Brown

1. Dr Ola Brown was born in London in 1986.

2. Dr Ola Brown attended Hull York Medical School and is the youngest-qualifying medical doctor on record.

3. Dr Ola Brown was fostered by a white family.

4. Dr Ola Brown established the Flying Doctors in Lagos in 2007,

which was West Africa's first air-operated medical emergency service.

5. Dr Ola Brown was motivated to start up the Flying Doctors after the loss of her sister.

Five Facts about Kimberly Anyadike

1. Kimberly Anyadike was born in Compton, California, in 1994.

2. Kimberly and her sister Kelly are both aviation pioneers.

3. As a 15-year-old African American girl, Kimberly was the youngest person to fly from coast to coast across the USA. No one of any race or gender has beaten her record.

4. Kimberly is an African American whose parents are Nigerian. Her surname Anyadike means "eye of the warrior" in the Igbo language.

5. Kimberly achieved her dream by attending an after-school pilot programme. She started the programme aged 12.

Quick Quiz

Name three great things Bessie Coleman did as a teenager:

1.

2.

3.

What did Kimberly Anyadike achieve aged 15?

What did Dr Ola Brown begin aged 15?

Have these stories inspired you?

If you would like to tell us which is you favourite story, kindly ask your parent/guardian to leave a review on Amazon or Goodreads.

www.ingramcontent.com/pod-product-compliance
Lightning Source LLC
Chambersburg PA
CBHW012005090526
44590CB00026B/3886